anythink

D0579260

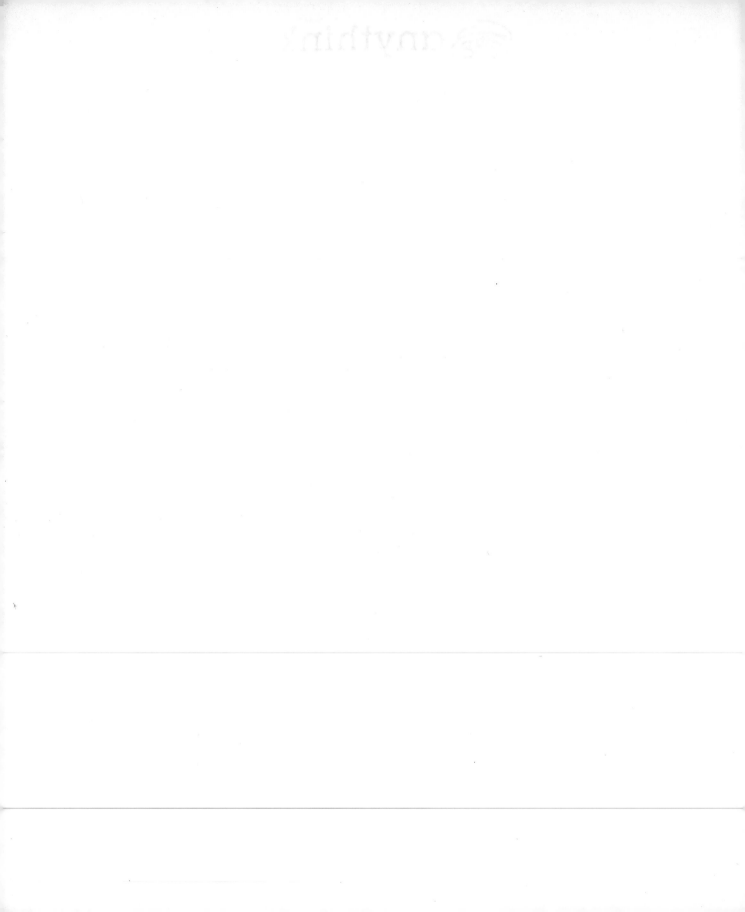

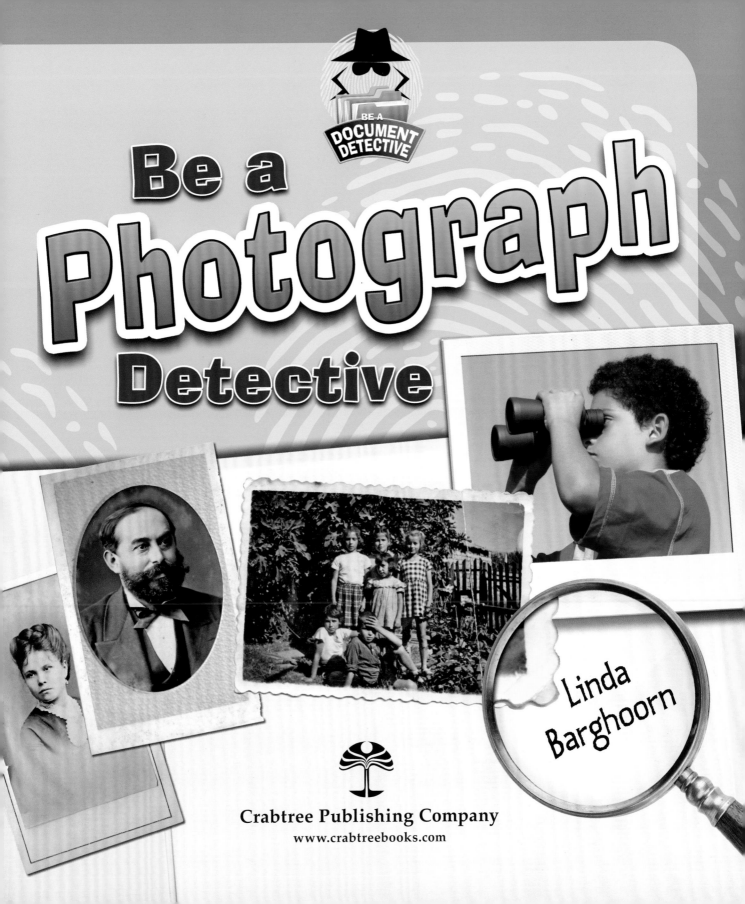

BE A
DOCUMENT DETECTIVE

Be a Photograph Detective

Linda Barghoorn

Crabtree Publishing Company
www.crabtreebooks.com

BE A
DOCUMENT DETECTIVE

Author: Linda Barghoorn

Series research and development: Reagan Miller

Editorial director: Kathy Middleton

Editors: Janine Deschenes, Reagan Miller

Proofreader: Petrice Custance

Design: Margaret Amy Salter

Production coordinator and prepress technician:
Margaret Amy Salter

Print coordinator: Margaret Amy Salter

Photographs:

Shutterstock: © KUCO, title page (center);
© gary718, p9 (bottom right); © Michael Rosebrock p 11;

Metras Museum: p 19 (bottom left)

United States Library of Congress: front cover (top left), p 17,
Wikimedia Commons: p19 (middle right)

All other images from Shutterstock

Library and Archives Canada Cataloguing in Publication

Barghoorn, Linda, author
        Be a photograph detective / Linda Barghoorn.

(Be a document detective)
Includes index.
Issued in print and electronic formats.
ISBN 978-0-7787-3066-8 (hardcover).--
ISBN 978-0-7787-3093-4 (softcover).--ISBN 978-1-4271-1872-1 (HTML)

        1. History--Research--Juvenile literature. 2. History--Sources--Juvenile
literature. 3. History--Methodology--Juvenile literature. 4. Photographs--
Research--Juvenile literature. 5. Photographs as information resources--
Juvenile literature. I. Title.

D16.155.B37 2017   j907.2   C2016-907109-X
                                             C2016-907110-3

Library of Congress Cataloging-in-Publication Data

Names: Barghoorn, Linda, author.
Title: Be a photograph detective / Linda Barghoorn.
Description: New York : Crabtree Publishing Company, 2017. |
    Series: Be a document detective | Includes index.
Identifiers: LCCN 2017007120 (print) | LCCN 2017008098 (ebook) |
    ISBN 9781427118721 (Electronic HTML) |
    ISBN 9780778730668 (reinforced library binding : alk. paper) |
    ISBN 9780778730934 (pbk. : alk. paper)
Subjects: LCSH: Photography in historiography--Juvenile literature.
Classification: LCC D16.155 (ebook) | LCC D16.155 .B37 2017 (print) |
    DDC 907.2--dc23
LC record available at https://lccn.loc.gov/2017007120

Crabtree Publishing Company

www.crabtreebooks.com   1-800-387-7650

Printed in Canada/062017/MA20170420

Published in Canada
Crabtree Publishing
616 Welland Ave.
St. Catharines, Ontario
L2M 5V6

Published in the United States
Crabtree Publishing
PMB 59051
350 Fifth Avenue, 59th Floor
New York, New York 10118

Published in the United Kingdom
Crabtree Publishing
Maritime House
Basin Road North, Hove
BN41 1WR

Published in Australia
Crabtree Publishing
3 Charles Street
Coburg North
VIC 3058

Contents

History Detectives

How do we know what life was like in the past? Using the right tools, we can discover clues about life long ago. This book will teach you how to ask and answer questions to learn about the past.

What is History?

History is the study of things that happened in the past. It tells us how people and places have changed over time. **Historians** are people who study history. Historians are like detectives. They look for clues to help answer questions about the past. Historians look for answers to questions such as:

- **How and why do communities change over time?**

- **How have important discoveries changed our world?**

Finding answers to these questions can help us better understand the world today.

What are Primary Sources?

Historians use primary sources to look for clues about the past. Primary sources are records created by people during a certain time in history. They give **eyewitness** information about people, places, and events.

An object, such as this bicycle, is a primary source. It shows us one way people traveled from place to place more than 100 years ago.

*Primary sources, such as this diary, provide a **first-hand account** of what life was like in the past.*

Historians study objects, diaries, photos, and other primary sources. They use what they learn as **evidence** to support their answers to questions about the past.

Photographs, such as this photo of a family, are primary sources. We can learn things from photos, such as the kinds of clothes people wore during a certain time in history.

Look and Learn!

Did you know the very first photograph was taken in 1826? Since then, some historians believe people have taken as many as 3.5 trillion photographs!

Photographs are primary sources that show how things looked in the past. Historians can use photographs to answer questions about the past. For example, the photo shown here can help us answer these questions:

What games did children play in the past?

What kinds of clothes did children wear?

A Snapshot in Time

A photograph provides a snapshot of only one moment in time, so it cannot tell the whole story. One photograph cannot give all the answers to our questions. Historians must use evidence from many different primary sources to answer questions about the past.

Photographs can give clues about jobs people had in the past.

Photographs can help us learn about important events that happened in the past.

Milkman

Macy's Thanksgiving Day Parade, November 25, 2010

How to be a Photograph Detective

Photograph detectives look carefully at all parts of the photograph. They look at the largest parts of the image as well as small details. A detail is a small part or feature of a larger thing.

Photograph detectives pay attention to details to look for clues to learn about people, places, and events shown in the photograph. Look at the photograph below. You might notice that it shows an old classroom. But it also includes details such as the answer the boy is writing on the chalkboard, and the pictures hanging on the wall.

Searching for Clues

Small details give clues about the people, places, and events in photographs. For example, signs and dates can tell us where or when the photograph was taken.

Clues can also be found in **captions**. A caption is made up of words that describe the people, place, or event shown in a photograph. They are often found beside or under photographs in newspapers and books. Captions may be written by the person who took the photo or by a newspaper writer.

Detective Duty!

Look closely at this photograph and read the caption. Can you find the clues that tell us where and when the photograph was taken, and what it shows?

DODGE CITY, USA – MAY 17, 2015: Platform of the train station

11

Studying Photographs

Photograph detectives study photographs to help learn about what life was like in the past. One way to begin studying a photograph is by asking the five W questions. Use these questions to study the photograph on page 13.

Who?
What?
Where?
When?
And Why?

- **Who** is in the picture?
- **What** is happening in the photograph?
- **Where** is the photograph taken? Describe the scene or setting.
- **When** was the photograph taken? What time of day or year was it?
- **Why** do you think the photograph was taken?

WHO?: There is an old fire truck and firemen on top of it.

WHAT?: The firemen look like they are trying to put out a fire in a building.

WHERE?: Tall buildings and a paved, or covered, road are clues that the photograph was taken in a city.

WHY?: We need to find out more. The building is on fire. Maybe the photographer wanted a picture of the fire for the newspaper.

WHEN?: The photograph looks old because it is in black and white. The fire engine is an old style. The firemen are wearing old uniforms.

Looking for Answers:

After studying the photograph, what other questions do you have? For example, you might wonder:

Did old fire engines like this one have sirens?
What color were fire engines during this time?

Searching for clues to help answer your questions is all part of being a photograph detective. You may need to look at other sources to answer your questions. You might look for answers by visiting a museum or library, or by asking an **expert**.

Detective Duty!

How would the scene in the photograph look different if it was taken today? How would it look the same?

Past and Present

Studying photographs can help us **compare** and **contrast** communities today with how they were in the past. This helps us understand how places change over time.

The photographs on these pages show the Manhattan Bridge in New York City. They give us clues about how the city has changed from the time the Manhattan Bridge was built over 100 years ago until today. As you study the photographs, ask yourself the five W questions: **WHO**, **WHAT**, **WHERE**, **WHEN**, AND **WHY**.

Look closely at the bridge in each photograph, and the buildings and streets around it. What has changed in each photograph? Has anything stayed the same?

2

Describe two differences you noticed when comparing these photographs. Name two details that have stayed the same. Share your answers with others.

Photograph 1

- This photograph shows a city with a bridge over the river.
- The bridge is being built.
- The photo is taken from above ground; maybe from another building nearby.
- The photo looks like it was taken many years ago. The buildings are not very tall. There are old boats on the river and an old car parked in the street.
- This photograph looks like it was taken to show the bridge being built.

Photograph 2

- This is a photograph of a large city beside a river with a bridge.
- We cannot see anything happening in this photo.
- This photo looks like it was taken from an airplane.
- This photo looks very new. There are many tall buildings and a modern bridge.
- This photograph almost looks like a postcard. It could be celebrating how big the city is.

Celebrating
Exciting Moments

Some photographs show exciting **firsts** in history. Orville and Wilbur Wright were American inventors. They spent many years trying to build the first airplane that could fly. On December 17, 1903 they were finally successful. Orville's history-making first flight lasted for about 12 seconds.

What clues can you find in this photograph to tell us more about this important event? Use the five W questions to help you.

Detective Duty!

Write a caption for this photograph as if you were the person who took it.

WHO?: There is a man standing near the plane and another one on the wings of the plane. They could be Orville and Wilbur Wright.

WHAT?: It looks like the plane is about to land because we can see its shadow on the ground.

WHEN?: The photo looks very old because it is in black and white. Also, the plane looks much different than the ones used today.

WHERE?: It looks like they are on a beach or in a field because there is sand and mud on the ground.

WHY?: This could be one of their attempts to fly their new airplane.

A Timeline

A photograph detective can create a **timeline** by studying many photographs of the same **subject**. A timeline places events in order from the past to the present. Timelines can help us learn about how a person, place, or event has changed over time.

These three photographs show women playing ice hockey during the last 100 years. Look for clues that help you put the photographs in order from past to present or oldest to newest. These questions might help you:

- **What are the women wearing?**
- **What kind of hockey equipment do they have?**
- **Where was the photograph taken?**
- **What other questions might help you find clues?**

FRONT ROW, left to right: Judy Millen, Jackie Deratney, Nancy Morrow. BACK ROW: Sue Peever, Andy Bakogeorge (coach), Carol Brown, Gail Faskin, Mary Ann Moss, Wendy Warwick, Dave Moshenko (coach), Barb Johnson.

Detective Duty!

Study the photographs and use the clues you find to help you place the photographs on a timeline. Compare your timeline with others. Discuss the clues you used to help you create your timeline. Did your friends use different clues?

Create a Timeline

Create a photo timeline of your life. Think about the important events in your life that you want to include. You can use photographs that you have taken and photos that others have taken of you. As you choose your photos, think about the ones that best tell the story of YOU.

Activity:

Your photos should help a future photograph detective learn about your life and what is important to you. These questions can help you choose photographs to include:

- **Who are the people most important to you?**
- **What hobbies or sports do you enjoy?**
- **Do you have any special awards you are proud of, such as a school award or a sports trophy?**
- **Do you have a photo of a special time spent with your family?**
- **Can you include a baby picture, a toddler picture, and a picture of you today to show how you have changed?**

After you have chosen your photos, put them in order from past to present. Attach the photos to a large piece of paper. Write a caption below each photograph to describe what the photograph shows and why it is important. Include the date each photo was taken if you know it.

Detective Duty!

Remember the five W questions from page 12? Do your captions help answer these questions?

Activity Wrap-Up!

Your photo timeline should provide a unique picture of your life. It is special because it is about YOU!

Share your timeline with your classmates. Ask them what they discovered about you from the photos you chose. Does their answer surprise you? What did you learn about yourself from this activity?

Congratulations!

You now have the tools to be a real photograph detective. Keep up the detective work as you gather clues to help you learn more about the past!

Learning More

There are many places you can visit to find out more about primary sources. Start with your local museum and library. Churches, community groups, and schools are also good places to find information.

These books and websites will help you learn more:

Books

Bruno Clapper, Nikki. *Learning about Primary Sources*. Capstone Press, 2015.

Fontichiaro, Kristin. *Find Out Firsthand: Using Primary Sources*. Cherry Lake Publishing, 2013.

Kalman, Bobbie. *Travel Then and Now.* Crabtree Publishing Company, 2014.

Websites

https://cct2.edc.org/PMA/image_detective/students.html
This website helps students build their photograph detective skills by asking questions and gathering clues.

www.learner.org/interactives/historical/index.html
This website lets you practice your document detective skills by studying different primary sources and answering questions about them.

www.eduplace.com/kids/socsci/ms/books/bke/sources/index.html
These links to primary source documents will help you learn more about what life was like in the past.

Words to Know

caption	Words written on or near a photograph that describe what the photo shows
compare	To look at two or more things and notice how they are the same
contrast	To look at two or more things and notice how they are different
evidence	Information that helps prove something is either true or false
expert	Someone who has special knowledge on a subject
eyewitness	A person who sees something happen and can tell us about it
first	Something that happens for the first time in history
first-hand account	A story or source, such as a diary, that came directly from someone who experienced or witnessed an event
historian	A person who studies past events
history	The study of past events
subject	The person or thing being described or shown
timeline	A graphic organizer used to show events in order from past to present

Index

About the Author:

Linda Barghoorn has been sharing stories—hers and others—for years. She has traveled the world taking photographs of many things, such as dramatic landscapes in South America. She is the author of several children's books and is working on a novel about her father's life.

24